DUCT TAPE

101 ADVENTUROUS IDEAS FOR ART JEWELRY FLOWERS WALLETS AND MORE

FOREST WALKER DAVIS

Quarry Books
100 Cummings Center, Suite 406L
Beverly, MA 01915

quarrybooks.com • www.craftside.net

© 2015 by Quarry Books

First published in the United States of America in 2015 by
Quarry Books, a member of
Quarto Publishing Group USA Inc.
100 Cummings Center
Suite 406-L
Beverly, Massachusetts 01915-6101
Telephone: (978) 282-9590
Fax: (978) 283-2742
www.quarrybooks.com
Visit www.craftside.net for a behind-the-scenes peek at our crafty world!

10 9 8 7 6 5 4 3 2 1

ISBN: 978-1-63159-016-0

Digital edition published in 2015
eISBN: 978-1-62788-323-8

Library of Congress Cataloging-in-Publication Data

Davis, Forest Walker.
  Duct tape : 101 adventurous ideas for art, jewelry, flowers, wallets, and more / Forest Walker Davis.
    pages cm
  ISBN 978-1-63159-016-0 (paperback) -- ISBN 978-1-62788-323-8 (digital edition)
  1. Tape craft. 2. Duct tape. I. Title.
  TT869.7.D38 2015
  745.59--dc23
                                        2014049094

Designed at Burge Agency

Printed in China

TO MY PARENTS, JIM AND CLARE
DAVIS, WHO WILL HOPEFULLY FORGIVE
ME SOME DAY FOR THIS ENTIRELY
INADEQUATE DEDICATION.

CONTENTS

FOREWORD

I know this has happened to you.

You spot it from across the store: perfect, bright, and colorful rolls, neatly stacked or playfully jumbled in an oversized bin. It's eye candy drawing you in, and the need to touch it overwhelms. At first you don't know what it is, but then after picking up a roll, you find yourself smiling. Ah, duct tape.

A second realization sinks in as you toss the roll into your shopping basket and head to the check-out counter—and this makes you chuckle. You're in a pharmacy! Along with the sunscreen and variety pack of bandages, you're buying a roll of hot pink duct tape—and for no apparent reason.

Duct tape is everywhere these days. Once, during an intense three hours of running errands, I came across it at the hardware store, the supermarket, my local toy store, and (yes) the pharmacy. It wasn't even on my list of to-do's. As a duct tape artist, its ubiquitous presence is extremely convenient. I may not even realize that I'm running low on a particular color or pattern until I accidentally walk down an aisle and see it.

Duct tape is a diverse medium for creativity. It can be used to make wallets, bags, banners, garments, jewelry, belts, and other accessories. It can be folded, cut, and molded into various shapes for 2-D or 3-D art. Duct tape can be a substitute for fabric, paper, markers, and paint. I've even witnessed someone trying to crochet with it. While most people would snicker, I silently cheered her on. (Go, lady, go!)

The projects in this book showcase the power of duct tape. Forest understands that it's not just an adhesive. Duct tape is meant to be played with, to be manipulated and fine-tuned, and to be transformed. There seems to be no limit to what a person can create, whether it's art or craft, or something in between. And you can be an old, married lady with kids or a young bachelor with the world at his feet. Forest and I are two very different people, but we shape our inspiration through duct tape. And because of this, we are kindred spirits.

—RICHELA FABIAN MORGAN

DUCT TAPE AS ART

I WISH I HAD A GOOD ORIGIN STORY. OTHER ARTISTS I KNOW CAN TALK ABOUT THE FIRST TIME SOMEONE GAVE THEM A PAINTBRUSH OR A CAMERA, ABOUT LEARNING TO SEE COLOR AND SHADOW AND LIGHT. "HOW DID YOU GET STARTED?" IS PROBABLY THE MOST COMMON QUESTION I GET ASKED, AND MORE THAN A DECADE LATER, I STILL DON'T HAVE A SATISFACTORY ANSWER. SOMETIMES I JOKINGLY REPLY THAT I WAS FOND OF GIRLS AND KNEW THAT I WOULDN'T BE ANY GOOD AT SPORTS, WHICH IS AT LEAST A LITTLE BIT TRUE.

A better answer is that I always had a creative orientation, was lucky enough to be the son of an art teacher and a musician, and ran into creative people in school who inspired and encouraged me.

I remember somewhere around eighth grade, it became vogue to make wallets and book covers with duct tape. My first wallet weighed about two pounds and had pockets everywhere, hiding notebooks and pencils and playing cards and a pocketknife, but this soon evolved into more portable models. The concept of transforming something blatantly utilitarian into something beautiful appealed to me, as it still does. When I realized that people were willing to pay me five or ten dollars for a duct tape flower, my interest was piqued, but I was (and still am) reluctant to make art for profit, preferring to make things because I feel like they need to be made.

The progression from first wallet through more and more complex artworks to the present day was so slow and gradual that sometimes it feels like one day I woke up like this, teaching art classes, writing a book, and making flowers for weddings. For this reason, it's sometimes hard to identify a starting point, or a decision that led me here, but it's a pretty nice place to be.

Duct tape occupies an odd place in the world of art. It is often put in an umbrella category such as "mixed media" or "novelty art," and much of the existing material on the subject is marketed toward teenagers, showing the un-seriousness with which it is generally regarded. This un-seriousness, however, is part of its appeal. It allows you, the artist, the freedom to make what you want to make in whatever way you'd like to make it. It's unpretentious and simple, a functional and utilitarian thing that people all over the world have elevated in beautiful and unexpected ways, like a gourmet hot-dog stand.

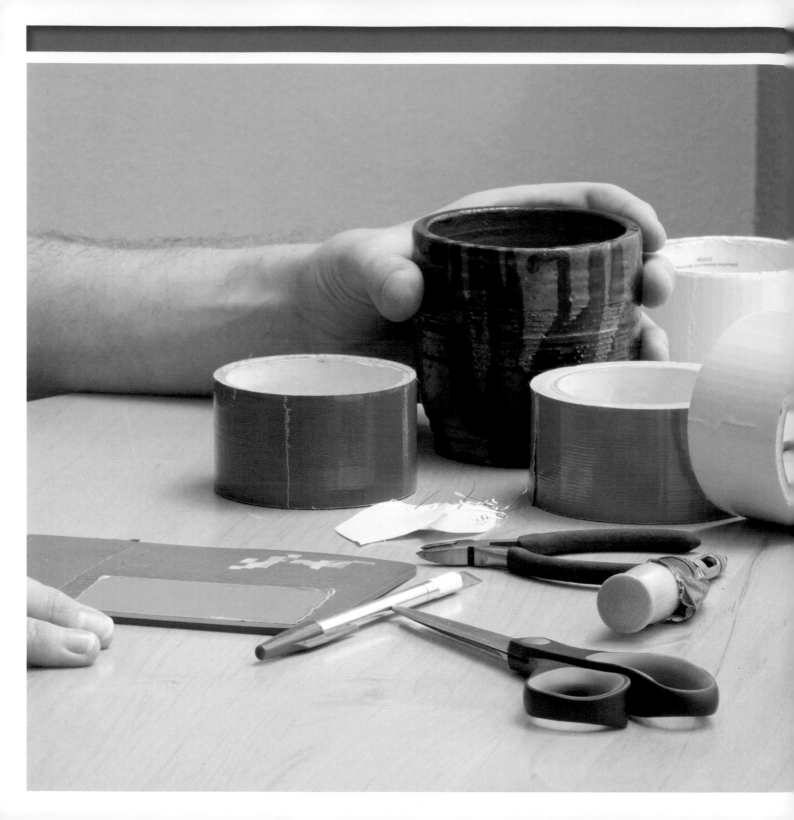

CHAPTER ONE

GETTING STARTED

ONE OF THE THINGS I ENJOY MOST ABOUT DUCT TAPE AS A MEDIUM IS THE ACCESSIBILITY —TAPE CAN BE FOUND AT VIRTUALLY ANY CORNER STORE AND ISN'T VERY EXPENSIVE COMPARED WITH OTHER ART MEDIA. IN THIS WAY, IT'S VERY DEMOCRATIC. MOST OF THE NON-TAPE MATERIALS ARE SIMILARLY AVAILABLE AND INEXPENSIVE, SO THE BARRIER TO ENTRY IS VERY LOW.

Another thing I like is that it can be done almost anywhere. I feel most comfortable making art in ooffoohoucoc and barc booauco I think it's probably good for me to have some human interaction, and I've made some good friends and professional contacts that I wouldn't have if I were in my basement working to the sounds of an old *Star Trek* episode. I try not to take up more space than I need, and if I'm occupying one of the few large tables, I'll put up a sign that says "nice people may sit here" so that I don't feel guilty about overstaying my welcome. It's a good idea to pick tables that are square or rectangular because circular tables make it difficult to make big sheets of tape for wallets and purses and the like. It's also good to find a table that has a smooth, unpainted surface because it gives you a place to set down your strips of tape as you're making them, and the adhesive can remove paint from tabletops, which can anger the owners of the coffeehouse or bar.

TOOLS

Most of the tools I use are simple ones, but I encourage you to use whatever resources you have access to and not feel limited by the manufacturer's intent. I recall one particular project in which I needed to carve large pieces of closed-cell foam into smooth shapes suitable for decorating with tape. My father, who inspects beehives, happened to have a specialized tool called a capping knife that looks a bit like an electrified garden trowel. The idea was that the knife would get warm and melt its way through the foam like a heated ice cream scoop. As it happens, this was not very effective, and I went back to using a steak knife. Go forth and find the things that work and learn from the things that don't. That being said, here are the tools I use most frequently.

CUTTING BOARD

I prefer a cutting board with some "give" to it, like the self-healing rubber mats available at most craft stores. The knife is better able to sever the strings of the tape if the blade can sink into the cutting board a bit. Avoid the hard plastic and wooden mats. Bigger is better.

HOLE PUNCH

Sometimes you will need to make circles. For smaller circles, a hole punch seems the obvious solution, but it stretches out the edges of the circle, so it just won't do. The best thing for smallish circles is a book drill or a screw punch. This wooden-handled tool with a cutting bit twists as you push it down, thus rendering a perfect circle. It comes with bits of various sizes. For larger circles, the craft knife is very effective.

SCISSORS

A good pair of scissors is essential, but the good ones aren't always the most expensive. I've purchased several pairs at dollar stores that outperformed those available at craft stores. A note regarding scissors: When they get clogged up with adhesive residue (and they will), take a small piece of tape and rub the sticky side very carefully along the blade of the scissors several times until the residue is removed. It's important to do this frequently to ensure cleaner cuts. I recently acquired a pair of Fiskars scissors designed for Duck brand to cut duct tape and other adhesives. I can attest that they work beautifully.

CRAFT KNIFE

Any brand of these knives will do fine, but I prefer the ones with metal handles over the plastic because they're less likely to break. I always carry extra blades, because they dull quickly and sometimes break. I don't have an official cover for mine, so I used a pen cap.

WIRE CUTTERS

My wire cutters are pretty simple things. You can find them at most craft stores. I bought a pair at a dollar store once, but they broke almost immediately. Be sure to oil them every now and again.

COFFEE

...and lots of it!

SKILLS

THE PROJECTS IN THIS BOOK REPRESENT A PRETTY WIDE SCALE OF DIFFICULTY, BUT EVEN THE EASIEST PROJECTS CAN BE DAUNTING WITHOUT A PRIMER OF THE ESSENTIAL SKILLS. IT MIGHT HELP IF YOU'RE VERY NEW TO DUCT TAPE TO PRACTICE TEARING AND FOLDING SOME SQUARES, JUST TO GET THE FEEL OF IT.

FOLDING TAPE

■ Keep your fingers out of the way.

■ Use the sides of the tape for guidance.

■ Always fold from the crease downward to avoid wrinkles. If you're folding a sheet of tape, always fold from the crease toward the open end.

TEARING TAPE

When tearing tape off the roll, first unwrap the desired length of tape. Next, hold the roll in your left hand and use your left index finger as the stopping point for your tape strip.

Last, grasp the free strip with your right hand close to your stopper-finger, and then thrust your right hand quickly downward using the pad of your thumb (pictured) as an edge. Alternatively, you can attach the tape end to the edge of your table, unroll it to the desired length, and then cut it with scissors while keeping the strip taut with the roll in your other hand. Tearing tape slowly may result in an uneven or stretched edge, so don't be afraid to tear with vigor and gusto.

MAKING SHEETS

When making sheets of tape for wallets, purses, or other big, flattish things, plan ahead so they don't come apart later. Lay your strips on your tabletop sticky-side up (SSU—an acronym I'll use occasionally in this book), overlapping each by about ¼ to ⅓ inch (6 to 8 mm). Next, complete your sheet by laying another layer of strips sticky-side down perpendicular to your first layer. Making your top layer perpendicular to your bottom layer keeps the overlaps from becoming too prominent, and provides added strength.

When you're overlapping the tape, you should touch them *lightly* with your fingers to seal the adhesive. When you're adding strips for the top layer, you'll want to have the center of the tape strip touch the bottom layer first, dropping your hands slowly to make sure the strip is evenly and smoothly applied.

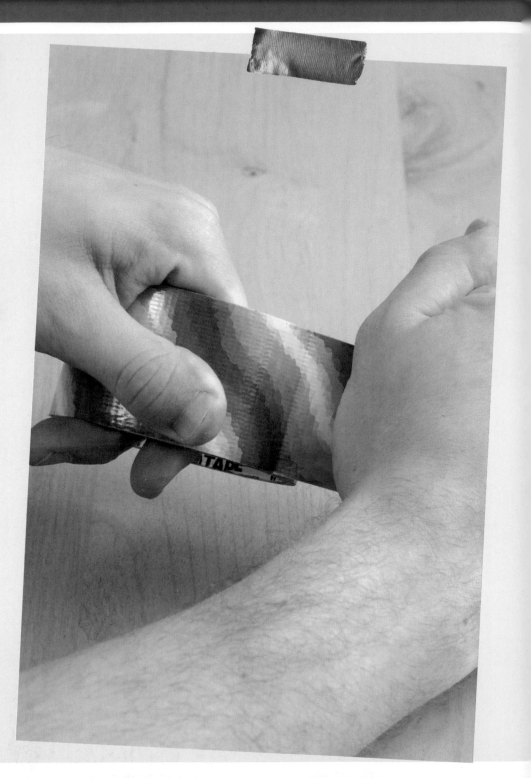

OTHER BEGINNING TIPS

I prefer to use Duck brand duct tape because of the quality of the tape and the variety of colors, but not all Duck brand tapes are the same! Some rolls have a pattern of perforations (which feel smoother), and some have a crossed-string pattern (which are more textured in appearance). You should look for the rolls with the crossed strings; they're easier to tear, and the edges are straighter than the perforated tape, which can form abrupt lateral rips when being torn.

Planning out your projects in stages can be a time-saver, especially when dealing with dozens of identical parts. It is easier, for example, to tear twenty strips, fold them, cut them, and apply them together rather than doing each one in turn. If you need nine strips of equal length for a wallet, you can measure the first, then stretch that one out in front of you, and measure the others against it. The same is true for wires and other materials.

More on planning: I like to sketch out my projects ahead of time to predict possible design problems. I have sent many colored pencils to their graves this way. It's true what they say about an ounce of prevention being worth a pound of cure: Nothing is worse than getting halfway through a "grand work" and having to restart because you didn't realize there was something wrong with the plan.

Newsprint is useful as a filler material, but newspapers are usually printed with an ink that smears when you crumple it, which can cause black smudging on your hands and spread to lighter-colored tapes. I noticed this on the sashimi especially. Before you use printed papers for duct tape art, crumple some between your fingers to see whether the ink shows up on your hands. If so, you might consider using a different paper.

There is often a lot of repetitious tedium, and it can be helpful to share the load by enlisting family, neighbors, and friends to assist in tearing or folding. You'd be surprised how much work can be bought with a beer or a coffee or a bar of chocolate.

CHAPTER TWO:
FLOWERS

I STARTED MAKING FLOWERS IN GRADE SCHOOL FOR MY FRIENDS. BACK THEN, THEY WERE EXTREMELY SIMPLE AND DIDN'T HAVE ANY WIRES IN THEM, SO THEY WEREN'T VERY DURABLE. IN COLLEGE, I STARTED SELLING THEM TO RAISE MONEY FOR THE ENVIRONMENTAL CLUB.

Though I've always had a deep, abiding love for biology and nature, I was (and still am) less concerned with botanical accuracy than with aesthetic sensibility and making stuff I think is interesting and challenging. I apologize to readers for the large portion of this book dedicated to flowers, but I hope you'll forgive me for the following reasons. First, nature constantly surprises me with a diversity of beauty and depth that artists could spend their whole lives emulating, as thousands of artists have. Second, the skills necessary in making flowers — namely, a sense of symmetry, an eye for proportion, and a lot of patience — will serve you well in every project you undertake.

THE FIRST PROJECT MOST PEOPLE LEARN, AND THE FIRST ONE I TEACH MY STUDENTS, IS THE POINT-PETAL ROSE. IT IS ONE OF THE OLD CLASSICS OF THE DUCT TAPE TRADE, IF SUCH A THING CAN BE SAID TO EXIST. I USE THE POINT PETALS IN JUST ABOUT EVERYTHING I DO, WHETHER A FLOWER OR NOT.

POINT-PETAL ROSE

WITH PRACTICE AND PLANNING, YOU CAN MAKE SPIRALS AND CONCENTRIC CIRCLES WITH ALTERNATING COLORS, OR EVEN SPIDERS AND EYEBALLS. THESE ARE PARTICULARLY FUN AND REWARDING WHEN YOU GET THEM RIGHT.

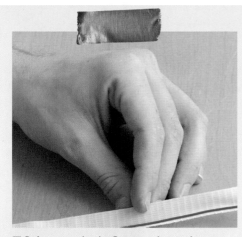

■ Before we make the flower, we have to have something to put it on. It can be anything at all, but we're going to use wire. Tear a piece of tape vertically, so that it's the same length as your wire, then roll the tape carefully around the wire, beginning at the edge.

■ First, you'll tear a series of squares. The completed flower will have anywhere between twenty and fifty petals, so that's how many squares you need, though it's not necessary to tear them all at once.

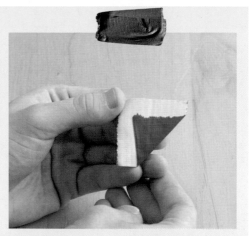

■ Next, take one corner of a square and fold it down so that it forms a right triangle region of smooth tape, with adhesive borders on two sides. The newly smooth section should be about 75 percent of the surface of the petal at this stage.

■ Take one corner and fold it along the hypotenuse of the triangle until it looks roughly house-shaped. The front of the petal should have a smooth triangular section with a rectangular section beneath. The opposite side should have no adhesive showing, and the point should be very slightly rounded, with a little loop on one side.

■ Hold your wire vertically in one hand and your petal in the other. Stick the petal to the end of the wire with the point sticking straight up and then roll it around the stem. The petal should be stuck high enough to keep the wire from showing, but low enough so that it doesn't flop around.

■ Repeat with subsequent petals, keeping the points either lined up at the top or very, *very* slightly increasing in height with each new level. If it looks like a cone, you're going up too fast; make sure the petals' tips are closer to the same height.

ROSE VARIATIONS

FROM LEFT TO RIGHT: HALF-SIZE PETALS, ARRANGED RANDOMLY; "ARTICHOKE-STYLE" CENTER WITH PENTAGONAL SYMMETRY; SQUARE SYMMETRY BICOLOR; AND TRICOLOR SPIRAL.

PLAIN LILY

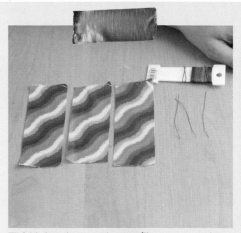

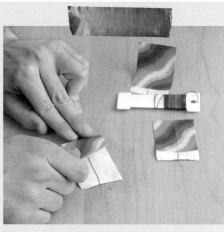

■ A lily has three petals, so we'll measure out three strips of equal length and three wires about half the length of the strips.

■ Placing the wire in the center of the tape, with the tip a little less than halfway down the length, carefully fold the tape over the wire, leaving some adhesive on the bottom and some space between the wire tip and the fold.

■ Cut the strip into a petal shape.

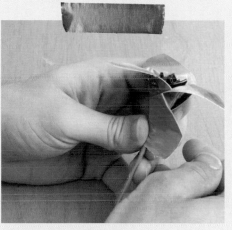

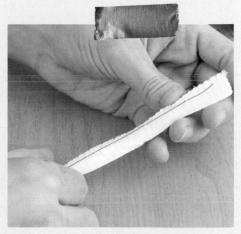

■ When your petals are cut, you'll place them on the stem, but first you need to make a flower center big enough to hold the petals. For this one, I used the point-petal style.

■ To finish, make a few extra point petals in the same color as your stem, and place them at the juncture of the flower and the stem, to cover up the seams and to make a smooth transition. In nature these are called sepals.

■ Lilies have lance-shaped, elongated leaves, so we'll fold a long piece of tape over a wire and cut out a point at the end.

TORN-STRIP LILY

INSTEAD OF CUTTING THE PETAL SHAPE
AND THEN DECORATING IT, I PLACED
TORN STRIPS ON THE FOLDED LENGTH
OF TAPE BEFORE I CUT IT, MAKING A
MORE NATURAL-LOOKING BOUNDARY

THIS FLOWER WAS MADE BY CUTTING VERY SMALL SQUARES, THEN FOLDING THEM INTO POINT PETALS, AND THEN PLACING THOSE POINTS ONTO AN UNCUT LILY PETAL (STILL IN THE RECTANGULAR STAGE). ONCE ALL THE POINTS WERE IN PLACE, I CUT THE SHAPE OF THE LILY PETAL, CREATING SHARPER EDGES THAN IF I HAD DONE THOSE TWO STEPS IN REVERSE. INITIALLY, I INTENDED TO MAKE ONE FLOWER FOR EACH OF THE EIGHT MAJOR HOUSES OF A POPULAR FANTASY NOVEL SERIES, BUT TO THIS DATE, I HAVEN'T GOTTEN PAST THE DRAGON.

SCALES LILY

SOMETIMES, IF I WANT MORE SURFACE AREA FOR DECORATION, I USE TWO STRIPS FOR EACH PETAL, WHICH MUST BE LENGTHENED TO ACCOUNT FOR THE PROPORTIONS. I CALL THIS DECORATION "THE EXPLODING PLANET," FORMED BY CUTTING A CIRCLE AND SLICING IT INTO BITS WITH A CRAFT KNIFE, AND THEN CAREFULLY PLACING EACH PIECE ON THE PETAL; I RETAIN THE CIRCULAR SHAPE BY EXPANDING ITS DIAMETER, ALLOWING THE UNDERLYING COLOR TO FILL IN THE NEGATIVE SPACE.

EXPLODED-PLANET LILY

TINY LILIES

I USUALLY FIND THAT THE
SMALLER YOU CAN MAKE
SOMETHING, THE COOLER IT
IS. THE INVERSE IS ALSO TRUE,
BUT IT WOULD TAKE A LOT OF
TAPE AND A VERY LONG TIME
TO MAKE A VIKING LONGSHIP
OUT OF DUCT TAPE.

IT TAKES LESS TIME TO MAKE THIS
STYLE OF ROSE THAN THE POINT-PETAL
ROSE AND LOOKS MORE REALISTIC, BUT
IT DEFINITELY TAKES SOME PRACTICE
TO GET THE HANG OF IT.

SMOOTH-PETAL ROSE

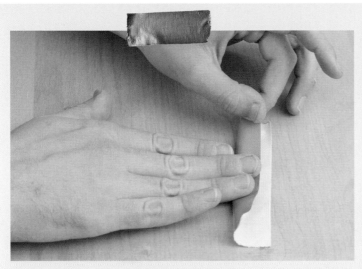

■ You'll need quite a few strips of tape between 2 and 6 inches (5 and 15 cm) long, folded along their length, with room for adhesive.

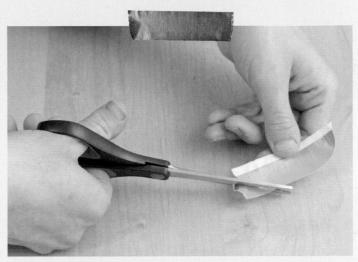

■ Then, cut the top corners off, making it as smooth as possible

■ Wrap the petals one by one around the stem (I started this with one point petal) so that some airspace is left between the outside edge of the petal and the stem. This is accomplished by pinching the bottom surface tight, while keeping the top surface loose.

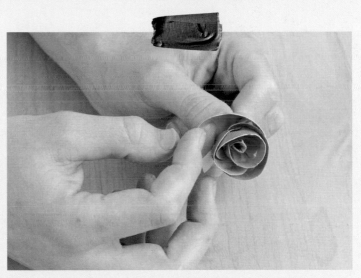

■ Continue adding petals so that the top of each new strip is roughly even with the previous petals.

THE SMALL BLUE ROSE HERE WAS MADE
WITH THE SAME TECHNIQUE AS THE LARGER
SMOOTH-PETAL ROSE, BUT WITH STRIPS ONE-
THIRD THE SIZE.

SMOOTH-PETAL ROSE VARIATION

THIS IS A CENTER-PUNCTURE FLOWER IN THE SHAPE OF A MELTED CLOCK, IN HOMAGE TO SALVADOR DALÍ'S PAINTING *THE PERSISTENCE OF MEMORY*. I HAVE A SPECIAL AFFECTION FOR FLOWERS THAT ARE ALSO OTHER OBJECTS, AND I HAVE ANOTHER SPECIAL AFFECTION FOR THE WORK OF DALÍ AND THE OTHER SURREALISTS.

MELTED CLOCK (CENTER PUNCTURE)

ORCHIDS ARE A LOT LIKE LILIES, BUT WITH
AN ODDLY IRREGULAR BOTTOM PETAL THAT
HAS TWO WIRES INSIDE. IT TOOK A LOT OF
PRACTICE TO GET THE SHAPE RIGHT.

ORCHID

THESE WATER LILIES BOTH FEATURE THE
SHORT-GRASS STYLE OF CENTER. THE LILY PAD
IS MADE BY LAYING SEVERAL STRIPS SSU (SEE
PAGE 18), THEN PLACING A COIL OF WIRE ON IT.
BEFORE SEALING IT IN WITH THE TOP LAYER OF
TAPE, POKE THE WIRE THROUGH THE CENTER
OF THE COIL SO THAT YOU CAN ATTACH THE
FLOWER, THEN SEAL IT AND CUT OUT THE LILY
PAD SHAPE.

WATER LILY

HIBISCUSES ARE ESSENTIALLY FIVE-PETALED
LILIES, AND BECAUSE THEY CREATE MORE
SURFACE AREA, THEY GIVE THE ARTIST A
LARGER CANVAS TO WORK WITH. THE CENTERS
OF ALL THREE OF THESE BEGIN WITH POINT
PETALS IN DIFFERENT PATTERNS, WITH
LANCES IN THE "DIGITAL" FLOWER AND CLASSIC
STAMENS IN THE YELLOW HIBISCUS. ALL THREE
FLOWERS ARE ALSO DECORATED WITH TAPE
CUT WITH A CRAFT KNIFE.

HIBISCUS VARIATIONS

THE FIRST FEW EYEBALL FLOWERS
HAD POINT PETALS INSTEAD OF
SMOOTH PETALS. I LIKE THIS BETTER.

EYEBALL FLOWER

I MADE A NUMBER OF TINY LILIES HERE, AND THEN AFFIXED THEM TO A CENTRAL POINT TO MAKE A COMPOUND FLOWER. I DIDN'T PUT WIRES IN ANY OF THE CREAM-COLORED PETALS TO SAVE TIME, BUT BECAUSE THE PETALS TEND TO CLOSE UP, IN RETROSPECT THE WIRES WOULD HAVE BEEN HELPFUL.

BIRD'S BEAK COMPOUND FLOWER

BONSAI

THIS IS A TYPE OF CENTER-PUNCTURE FLOWER WHERE EACH CIRCULAR FLOWER IS CUT ROUGHLY OUT OF A SMOOTH STRIP, THEN DECORATED WITH SEVERAL COLORS CUT WITH THE CRAFT KNIFE. THE WIRE IS THEN POKED THROUGH THE CENTER AND A SMALL PIECE OF YELLOW TAPE IS PLACED OVER THE WIRE AND CUT INTO A LANCE SHAPE TO KEEP THE FLOWER FROM SLIPPING OFF THE WIRE. THIS ONE HAS MORE THAN FIFTY FLOWERS, THE SMALLEST OF WHICH ARE SMALLER THAN A PENCIL ERASER. YOU COULD MAKE A TREE LIKE THIS WITH LEAVES OR FRUIT INSTEAD OF FLOWERS IF YOU WISH.

COMPOUND CENTER-PUNCTURE FLOWER

THIS ONE IS SIMILAR TO THE BONSAI FLOWER, BUT ALL THE WIRES EMANATE FROM A SINGLE POINT. THE FLOWERS ARE KEPT AT THE END OF THE WIRE BY BUNCHING THE WIRE SLIGHTLY BEHIND THE PETAL. YOU COULD ALSO DO THIS WITH A DAB OF TAPE.

ARTICHOKE CENTER

This is what I call an "artichoke." It's made by slightly lowering the level of each layer of point petals.

LONG ROLL CENTER

This is a "long roll". Tear an extra-long strip of tape, fold it lengthwise (leaving a little room at the bottom edge for adhesive), then carefully roll it around a wire until you've got the proper thickness. I like this one for daisies.

SHORT-GRASS CENTER

For a short-grass center, fold a strip of tape on its width like the smooth-petal rose, then cut deep triangles out of the smooth side until they look like grass. It takes a while, but it's a useful thing for texture (see the fox on page 103).

LONG-GRASS CENTER

The long-grass center is like the short grass, but the strip is folded lengthwise like a lily petal. It's also good for things besides flowers.

DRAGON TONGUE CENTER

I call these "dragon's tongues," not for any good reason but because I needed to call them something. They're basically long grass with a V cut in the top.

BUTTERFLY TONGUE CENTER

Butterfly tongues are a thin strip of tape wrapped around a wire, then coiled. I like the look of them, but they have a tendency to unravel after a while. I haven't come up with a perfect solution, but trying to wrap them loosely seems to work okay.

LANCE CENTER

I like to make these out of silver or gold tape, and if you've got a few flowers with this center in a bouquet, it looks particularly fancy.

SPIRAL CENTER

I made this with a coil of wire on a small sheet of SSU tape, cut it out in a spiral pattern, and then decorated it with cut strips.

CLASSIC STAMEN

I call these "classic stamens" because they most closely resemble the pollen-producing structures in most flowers. It's a wire, usually covered with tape, with a strip of bright-colored tape on top.

WHEAT STALK CENTER

I am particularly fond of these, which I call "wheat stalks." They're similar to the artichoke center, but with each successive layer dropped farther down.

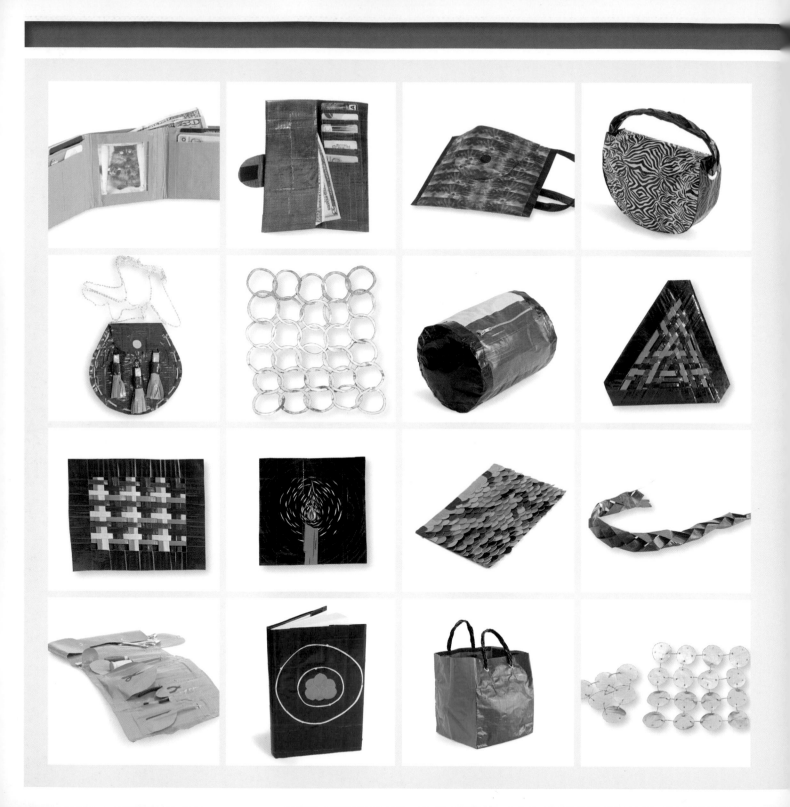

CHAPTER THREE

WALLETS, PURSES, BAGS, AND MORE

THE PROJECTS IN THIS CATEGORY ALL REQUIRE MAKING LARGE SHEETS OF TAPE, OR ELSE THEY'RE MEANT FOR USE WITH PROJECTS INVOLVING LARGE SHEETS OF TAPE. THIS OFTEN MEANS YOU'LL HAVE A WORKSPACE COVERED WITH A SURFACE OF STICKY TAPE, WHICH CAN BIND TOGETHER WITH ONE WRONG MOVE. TAKE YOUR TIME, AND ASK FOR HELP IF YOU NEED AN EXTRA HAND.

There are lots of ways to fasten your wallets, purses, boxes, and bags, which may require purchasing special materials such as adhesive-backed Velcro strips, snaps, grommets, or buckles. None of these are very expensive or terribly difficult to Install, though the grommets and snaps require a hammer.

THE FIRST THING, OTHER THAN THE POINT-PETAL ROSE,
THAT MOST PEOPLE LEARN TO MAKE IS THE WALLET.
IT COMES IN MANY FORMS, FROM A SIMPLE BI-FOLD
ENVELOPE TO A SWISS ARMY-STYLE MULTI-TOOL
WITH FIFTY POCKETS THAT UNFOLD LIKE A LOTUS.
WE'RE GOING TO TRY FOR THE MIDDLE GROUND HERE.

BASIC WALLET

■ My wallet starts with nine strips of tape, an odd number because it places the folds in the centers of the strips, rather than the overlaps. For a shorter wallet, use seven strips and for a taller wallet, eleven.

■ Carefully fold the near and far edges into the center. If this results in a sticky gap, fill it in with a small strip of tape.

■ Form an envelope by folding in half. Using scissors, cut one side so that it's straight and even, then from this edge fold the wallet either in thirds or in half, just to get a sense of how big it's going to be. Cut the remaining side when you're confident it's the right length.

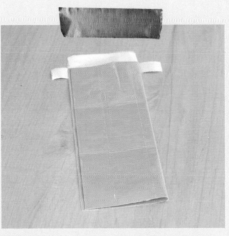

■ When the wallet is as long as you'd like it, cut a strip somewhat longer than the height of your wallet, and place one side of the wallet along it like this.

■ Cut out the corners as shown and fold the flaps over to seal the front and back of the wallet together. Repeat with the other edge.

■ Fold and cut some panels for pockets. Make them slightly smaller than the wallet segment, then seal them with a few strips on three sides and excise the remainder.

■ The completed wallet, with a clear plastic panel for photographs and someone else's money.

My first wallet had a pocket on the side that contained a playing card wrapped with several feet of duct tape for emergencies (broken glasses, a hole in the shoe, etc.). I don't recommend using a playing card because the last few inches will stick to the cardboard and become useless, but a piece of plastic with a few yards of tape is something I think everyone should have on his or her person.

VERTICAL WALLET

I MADE THIS IN THE SAME MANNER AS THE BASIC WALLET, BUT WITH DIFFERENT MEASUREMENTS. THE LEFT HALF OF THE WALLET CONTAINS A POCKET, SO YOUR STARTING SHEET OF SMOOTH TAPE (I.E., AFTER THE SEALING LAYER IS APPLIED TO THE SSU TAPE) SHOULD BE THREE WALLET-WIDTHS WIDE, AND THEN ANOTHER WIDTH OR TWO FOR THE POCKETS, DEPENDING ON HOW MANY YOU WANT. IT'S HELD TOGETHER WITH AN ADDITIONAL ROUNDED FLAP AND A SQUARE OF VELCRO. YOU CAN ALSO MAKE A CHECKBOOK IN THIS WAY.

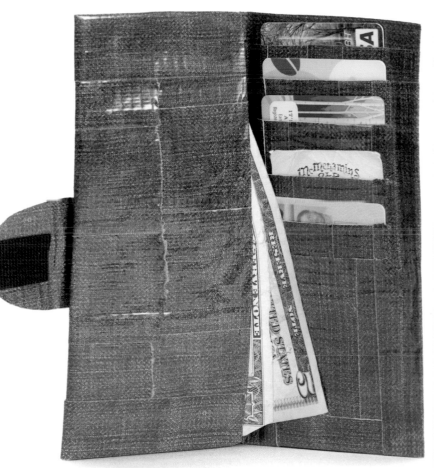

The completed bag's cover flap
attaches to the bag with Velcro
and is decorated with a small
circle for a fake button.

BASIC PURSE

■ The basic purse is a front panel and a back panel, with a strap and a flap to cover the opening. More complicated versions employ different kinds of side panels for more storage capacity, pockets, and so on, but they all begin with a sheet of tape.

■ I used blue tie-dyed tape for the bottom sheet and covered it with perpendicularly placed orange tie-dyed tape for the top sheet.

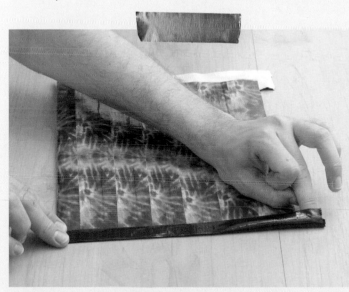

■ The edges were sealed with a strip of black.

■ I attached the strap as far along its length as possible to the entire inside edge of the purse, which gives the bag some strength and makes it less likely for the strap to come out.

ROUND PURSE

THIS ROUND PURSE IS MADE UP OF
A FRONT AND A BACK THAT WERE
MEASURED AND CUT TOGETHER TO
MAKE THEM IDENTICAL, EXCEPT FOR THE
CLOSING FLAP, WHICH IS AN INTEGRAL
PART OF THE BACK PANEL. THE FRONT
AND BACK ARE CONNECTED WITH A
THIRD CONTINUOUS SIDE PANEL, WHICH
IS SEALED ON THE INSIDE AND OUTSIDE
WITH MANY SMALL STRIPS OF TAPE.
ALSO, WHEN THE BRAIDED STRAPS ARE
PULLED AND STRETCHED TIGHT, AS SEEN
HERE, THEY HAVE A DIFFERENT LOOK
THAN THE SMOOTH BRAIDED STRAP
SEEN ON PAGE 62.

SPORRAN VARIANT OF ROUND PURSE

THE SPORRAN IS A TRADITIONAL PURSE CARRIED BY KILT-WEARING SCOTS AND IRISHMEN. I WAS INSPIRED TO MAKE THIS VARIATION ON THE ROUND PURSE AFTER ATTENDING A BURNS SUPPER AT THE HOME OF A SCOTTISH FRIEND. NOTICE HOW THE FRONT AND BACK PANELS ARE SEWN TOGETHER WITH DUCT TAPE THREAD.

BEACH BAG

THE BEACH BAG STARTED WITH A CROSS SHAPE FORMED BY SSU STRIPS IN TWO PERPENDICULAR DIRECTIONS. I THEN COVERED THEM CROSSWISE WITH SSU STRIPS, THEN BROUGHT THE SIDES UP INTO A BOX SHAPE. IT'S BEST IF YOU MEASURE THE BOTTOM OF THE BAG TO FIT OVER AN ACTUAL CARDBOARD BOX, SO THAT YOU CAN USE IT TO FORM THE CORNERS. IF YOU DON'T, YOU'LL BE FORCED TO AWKWARDLY TRY TO JOIN THE EDGES TOGETHER OVER THE BACK OF A CHAIR OR ENLIST THE AID OF A YOUNGER BROTHER OR HELPFUL NEIGHBOR.

RAINBOW ROUND BAG WITH ZIPPER

I WANTED TO MAKE SOMETHING WITH A ZIPPER, AND I WANTED IT TO BE ROUND. BEYOND THAT, THIS WAS AN EXPERIMENT WITH AN UNKNOWN CONCLUSION. I USED THREE STRIPS OF EACH COLOR, LAID THEM SSU, AND COVERED THEM WITH A NEUTRAL COLOR CROSSWISE. ONCE I'D CUT THE EDGES OFF AND EVENED IT OUT, I ROLLED IT UP INTO A TUBE, AND SET ABOUT LOOKING FOR A CYLINDER OF APPROXIMATE SIZE (A BUCKET, COOKING POT, JAR, ETC.) TO ACT AS A FORM. IF I MADE THIS AGAIN, I'D FIND A FORM CYLINDER AND THEN CUT THE TAPE TO THE RIGHT LENGTH. I MADE THE SIDES SLIGHTLY LARGER THAN THE OPENINGS, AND THEN CUT SLITS ALL THE WAY AROUND THE EXCESS, FOLDING THE "WINGS" UP AND THEN TAPING THEM DOWN. I'D USE A SMALLER VERSION OF THIS BAG DESIGN AS A PENCIL CASE, OR THE FULL-SIZE VERSION TO STORE MY LEGO BLOCKS, IF I STILL HAD ANY.

PURSE PANEL VARIATIONS

THESE FEW PICTURES DEMONSTRATE SOME OF THE DIFFERENT WAYS YOU CAN WEAVE PANELS FOR YOUR PROJECTS, ESPECIALLY PURSES AND BAGS. THERE ARE MANY MORE, I'M SURE, THAT THE DILIGENT TAPE ARTIST WILL DISCOVER WITH EXPERIMENTATION. AS FOR THESE, THE 1X1 WEAVE IS CERTAINLY THE SIMPLEST.

If you're worried about strength, you can put a wire in the strips before you fold them. Always make your woven panels larger than you think they'll need to be, first because there's some shrinking in the assembly, and second because it's always easier to cut excess than to try to make extensions. The hardest one for me to figure out was the triangle. It would probably have been easier with wide, flat strips rather than the small, thin ones I used.

■ purse panel variation, triangle

■ purse panel variation, thin-thick

■ purse panel variation, 2x1

■ purse panel variation, 1x1

BALLA'S CANDLE

THIS PANEL OF A CANDLE ILLUSTRATES THE KIND OF DECORATION YOU CAN MAKE ON A PURSE OR BAG WITH A CRAFT KNIFE AND A CUTTING BOARD. THIS PARTICULAR ONE WAS INFLUENCED BY A PAINTING CALLED *STREET LIGHT* BY THE ITALIAN FUTURIST PAINTER GIACOMO BALLA.

SCALE AND FISH SCALE PURSE PANEL

THESE ARE TWO OF MY FAVORITE DECORATIONS FOR PURSES. IT'S VERY TIME-CONSUMING, BUT IT LOOKS GREAT IN THE FINISHED PRODUCT. PLUS, IF YOU PLAN AHEAD AND ARE CAREFUL ABOUT PLACEMENT, YOU CAN MAKE INTERESTING DESIGNS USING THE POINTS AS PIXELS. THE ROUNDED SCALES ARE MORE FRAGILE THAN THE POINT PETALS, SO IT'S A GOOD IDEA TO EITHER STOP THEM 1 TO 2 INCHES (2.5 TO 5 CM) ABOVE THE BASE OR SEAL THE LAST LAYER WITH A COAT OF CLEAR TAPE TO AVOID SQUISHING.

The completed braid, with placeholder strips on each end to keep it steady until it's ready to be attached to a bag or purse.

BRAIDED STRAP

■ The braided strap begins as braids do, with three strips arranged next to each other and taped to the table to keep them in place while working. When the strap is completed, you'll go back and correct these first few inches to make them consistent with the rest of the braid.

■ Move two strips to the side, then bring the outermost strip in the pair to the middle, turning it a half turn as you do so.

■ Repeat the process using the outermost strip from the opposite side.

■ Continue this process, creasing the tape along the line of the braid as you bring each strap into the center.

TOOL ROLL

I HAD SEVERAL SUGGESTIONS FROM FRIENDS TO MAKE A TOOL ROLL, AND BECAUSE I HAVE AN ABUNDANCE OF WIRES, KNIVES, SCISSORS, AND EARRING BACKS, IT MADE SENSE FOR MY OWN PERSONAL USE AS WELL. THIS ONE IS ABOUT 24 INCHES (61 CM) LONG, COMPOSED OF FOUR FOLDED-UP SECTIONS. IF I DID THIS AGAIN, I WOULD MAKE SURE THAT THE BOUNDARIES OF THE POCKETS FALL NEATLY INTO THE CREASES OF THE FOUR SECTIONS, TO AVOID WRINKLING. EACH OF THE POCKETS HAS ITS OWN COVER, WHICH IS SECURED WITH A BIT OF VELCRO. THE OUTER FLAPS, WHICH PREVENT ANYTHING FROM FALLING OUT OF IT ONCE IT'S FOLDED UP, ARE SECURED WITH SNAPS.

BOOK COVER

I MADE THIS BOOK COVER BY MAKING A LONG SHEET OF SMOOTH TAPE SEVERAL INCHES TALLER AND LONGER THAN I THOUGHT I WOULD NEED (TO BUFFER IN CASE OF MISTAKES). YOU'LL WANT TO CUT THE TAPE WHILE IT'S FOLDED AROUND THE SPINE OF THE BOOK, OR IT MAY COME UP SHORT. THIS ONE IS DECORATED WITH AN ATOM BECAUSE IT'S A SCIENCE BOOK. (APOLOGIES TO SCIENTISTS FOR USING THE BOHR MODEL OF AN ATOM—I WOULD HAVE PREFERRED A PROBABILITY CLOUD, BUT THAT SEEMED LIKE AN AWFUL LOT OF WORK WITH THE RAZOR BLADE.)

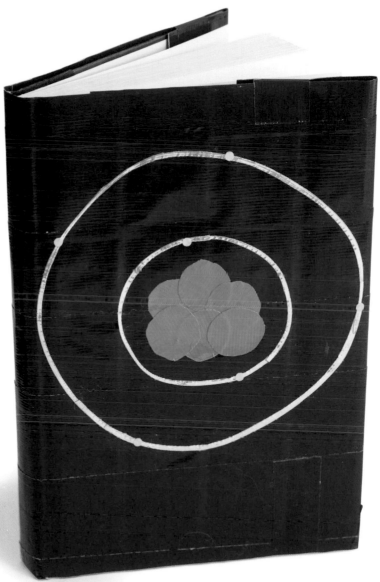

CHAINMAIL

CHAINMAIL IS, BELIEVE IT OR NOT, ONE OF THE MORE DIFFICULT PROJECTS IN THIS BOOK. MY FIRST FEW ATTEMPTS FAILED FROM BEING TOO SMALL OR FROM NOT CONNECTING THEM PROPERLY. I CUT ALL THE CIRCLES OUT AT THE SAME TIME, SO THAT I COULD ENSURE THEY WERE THE SAME SIZE, AND THE ACT OF CUTTING THE CENTER OUT OF THE RING NECESSITATED MAKING A SLIT IN THE SIDE OF THE RING FOR ACCESS. I FIRST TRIED TO CUT THE CIRCLE OUT WITH A CRAFT KNIFE TO AVOID HAVING TO PATCH THE CUT IN THE SIDE OF THE RING, BUT THAT WORKED POORLY. IT'S EASIER IF YOU TAPE THE RINGS TO YOUR WORKSPACE TO KEEP THEM FROM MOVING AROUND, AND BE SURE TO TAPE EACH RING CLOSED BEFORE APPLYING THE NEXT RING.

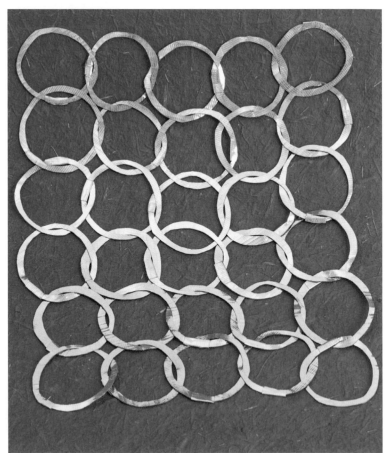

PLATE MAIL

THE CIRCULAR PLATES IN THE RECTANGULAR EXAMPLE ARE JOINED WITH FISHING LINE; THE PLATES IN THE TRIANGULAR EXAMPLE ARE JOINED WITH WIRE. I COULD SEE THIS TECHNIQUE BEING USED FOR HEADDRESSES, STREAMERS, BRACELETS, AND MANY OTHER THINGS. WITH THE FISHING LINE, IT WAS SURPRISINGLY SIMPLE.

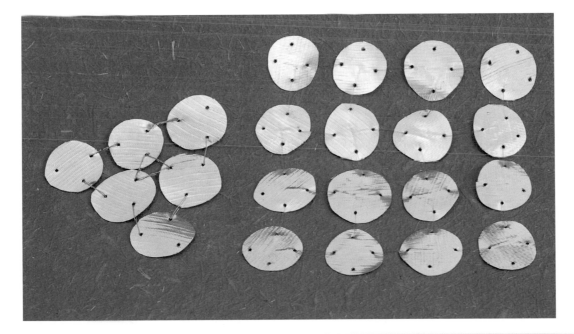

CHAPTER FOUR:
JEWELRY AND OTHER ACCESSORIES

EARRINGS ARE AMONG MY FAVORITE PROJECTS BECAUSE THEY DEMAND A LOT OF CONCENTRATION AND ATTENTION TO DETAIL, AND BECAUSE I CAN MAKE ABOUT 700 EARRINGS WITH THE AMOUNT OF TAPE THAT A BLAZER JACKET MIGHT REQUIRE. DUCT TAPE IS ESPECIALLY WELL SUITED TO THIS BECAUSE IT'S LIGHTER THAN MOST MATERIALS USUALLY USED FOR EARRINGS, WHICH MEANS YOU COULD WEAR A LARGER DUCT TAPE EARRING THAN A METAL OR WOOD EARRING WITHOUT ADDITIONAL DISCOMFORT.

I like to use a higher-quality silver-plated wire for these than I would normally use for duct tape art. You should try to get a smaller gauge, because the larger gauges are harder to twist. Many of these projects involve special backings, such as pins, clips, chains, and the like, which can be purchased at craft stores.

WIRE-FRAME EARRINGS, SNOWFLAKE

A SIMPLE WIRE FRAME IS THE EASIEST WAY TO MAKE EARRINGS OUT OF DUCT TAPE. FIRST, THREAD A WIRE THROUGH THE EARRING BACK, PULL A LOOP, AND TWIST SEVERAL TURNS TO CREATE A FEW MILLIMETERS DISTANCE BETWEEN THE EARRING BACK AND THE BEGINNING OF THE WIRE FRAME. NEXT, FORM THE WIRE INTO A CIRCLE (OR OTHER SHAPE). FINISH BY FOLDING A PIECE OF TAPE AND CUTTING THE EXCESS AROUND THE WIRE FRAME.

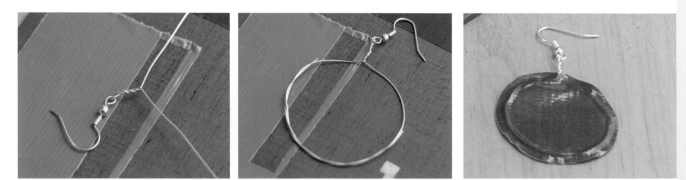

WIRE-FRAME EARRINGS, GALAXY

I THINK A LOT ABOUT QUESTIONS OF SCALE, SO I MADE THIS PAIR OF EARRINGS WITH A PICTURE OF A GALAXY ON ONE SIDE AND "HUME SWEET HOME" ON THE OTHER SIDE. DON'T TRY TO USE IT TO FIND YOUR WAY BACK IF YOU GET LOST IN OUTER SPACE, HOWEVER.

The finished earrings should look something like this.

CALLA LILY EARRINGS

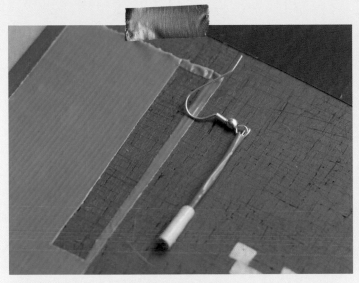

■ Calla lily earrings are my favorite kind, and consist of two parts. The first part is the stem, which starts with a piece of wire threaded through an earring back, wrapped with green tape, and topped with a piece of colorful tape, like yellow or orange.

■ The second part is the petal or hood, which involves a small lily petal shape with a wire. I usually make mine with a half-strip width and decorate them with cut pieces.

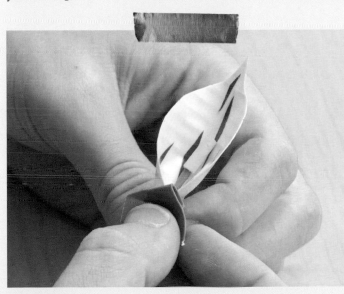

■ Carefully wrap the petal around the stem and seal it with one or two point petals.

SUNFLOWER EARRINGS

THE SUNFLOWER EARRINGS ARE A COMBINATION OF THE POINT-PETAL ROSE AND THE LILY, WRIT SMALL. IT IS IMPORTANT TO MAKE THE OUTER PETALS A UNIFORM SIZE, SO IT'S A GOOD IDEA TO CUT ALL THE WIRES AND TAPE STRIPS YOU'LL NEED BEFORE YOU START FOLDING AND SHAPING. IF YOU MAKE THE WIRES JUST A LITTLE BIT LONGER THAN THE PETALS, THERE'LL BE SOME LEFT OVER TO WRAP AROUND THE STEM AND SEAL WITH THE SEPALS, GIVING IT MORE STRENGTH.

DNA EARRINGS

THE DNA EARRINGS IN THIS BOOK ARE MY NINTH ATTEMPT TO MAKE THEM. I TRIED VERSIONS WITH PIECES OF TAPE WRAPPED AROUND WIRE, BUT THE EDGES OF THE TAPE UNRAVELED AFTER A WHILE, SO I SETTLED ON TAPE FOLDED OVER THE WIRE RATHER THAN WRAPPED. SOME OF THE VERSIONS HAD THE EDGES OF THE HELIX WRAPPED WITH TAPE, SOME DIDN'T. SOME HAD THE NUCLEOTIDES ATTACHED TO THE EDGES WITH WIRE, SOME WITH TAPE. ANYHOW, THESE ARE REALLY HARD AND I WELCOME WHATEVER SOLUTIONS YOU, THE DILIGENT READER, MIGHT COME UP WITH.

FEATHER EARRINGS

FEATHERS COME IN MANY SHAPES, BUT THE ONES I MAKE GENERALLY ARE ROUNDED AT THE TOP, HAVE SMALL CUTS IN THE SIDES TO INDICATE SEPARATIONS AND MAKE IT LOOK MORE LIFELIKE, AND THE LEFT AND RIGHT SIDES STAGGERED SLIGHTLY AS THEY MEET THE BASE. SOMETIMES I MAKE SEVERAL FEATHERS FOR EACH EAR.

NECKLACE

THE DESIGN FOR THIS NECKLACE
WAS INSPIRED BY A STONE MOSAIC,
AND IS VERY SIMILAR IN STRUCTURE
TO THE WIRE-FRAME EARRINGS,
EXCEPT FOR THE LARGE LOOP AT THE
TOP, WHICH LEAVES ROOM FOR THE
NECKLACE CHAIN.

IT TOOK SEVERAL TRIES TO FIND A SUITABLE METHOD FOR ATTACHING THE BUTTERFLY BODY TO THE PIN BACKING, AND FOR ATTACHING THE WINGS TO THE BODY. I SETTLED ON TYING THE BODY DOWN WITH WIRE, AND COVERING THE WIRES WITH TAPE, BUT YOUR METHODS AND RESULTS MAY VARY. THE WIRE FROM EACH WING WAS THREADED AROUND AND UNDER THE BODY, THEN TAPED TO THE UNDERSIDE OF THE OPPOSITE WING. THE CIRCLES WERE FORMED WITH THE HOLE PUNCH, AND RATHER THAN CUT OUT EACH YELLOW SECTION, I DECIDED TO CUT FOUR YELLOW SECTIONS (TWO FOR EACH WING) AND CREATE THE DIVISIONS IN THE SCALES BY OVERLAYING BLACK STRIPS.

BUTTERFLY PIN

MY FIRST ATTEMPT AT A BOW TIE WAS A LONG STRIP OF TAPE CUT TO THE PROPER SHAPE, BUT I FOUND THAT WHEN I TRIED TO TIE IT, THE RIGIDITY MADE IT DIFFICULT, AND IT DIDN'T LOOK RIGHT AT ALL. THE SOLUTION I CAME UP WITH WAS TO MAKE IT PRE-TIED, WITH PIECES OF VELCRO ON THE STRAP TO ADJUST THE SIZE.

BOW TIE

NECKTIE

ALTHOUGH THIS MAY LOOK LIKE I'VE MADE A LONG STRIP OF TAPE FABRIC AND TIED IT INTO THE CLASSIC SHAPE, I HAVE NOT. I MADE THE DANGLING PART AND THE KNOT AND THE NECK PART SEPARATELY. I WAS CONCERNED ABOUT IT BEING THICK AND HEAVY ENOUGH TO HOLD ITSELF DOWN, RATHER THAN CURLING UP OR CREASING AS A SINGLE LAYER MIGHT, SO I WENT OVER IT WITH SEVERAL LAYERS OF WHITE TAPE COVERED WITH PATTERNED TAPE. THE NECK PART CONNECTS TO THE KNOT WITH VELCRO.

HAIR BOW

THIS STARTED AS A TALL-ISH SHEET OF TAPE, CAREFULLY FOLDED AND CREASED AND THEN CRIMPED IN THE MIDDLE. I DISCOVERED THROUGH TRIAL AND ERROR THAT IT'S BEST TO MAKE IT A LITTLE "TALLER" THAN YOU THINK IS NECESSARY, BECAUSE IT SHRINKS IN THE FOLDING.

STRAIGHT BELT

HERE WE HAVE TWO EXAMPLES OF BELTS, AND TWO KINDS OF BUCKLES. FOR THE STRAIGHT BELT, I MEASURED ONE OF MY BELTS AND LAID OUT TWO STRIPS OF TAPE OF THAT LENGTH SSU. THEN, I FOLDED THE EDGES IN TO GET THE PROPER WIDTH, AND COVERED IT WITH TWO MORE STRIPS OF LENGTHWISE TAPE TO GET THE RIGHT THICKNESS. THE HOLES WERE MADE WITH MY SCREW PUNCH, BUT IF YOU WANTED THE BELT TO LAST LONGER, YOU COULD USE GROMMETS.

BRAIDED BELT

A BASIC BRAID IS DISCUSSED IN THE BRAIDED STRAP PROJECT ON PAGE 62.
THIS BRAIDED BELT IS A FIVE-WAY BRAID, WHICH WAS VERY CHALLENGING.
I FOUND INSTRUCTIONS ONLINE, AND ONCE I GOT THE HANG OF IT, IT WAS
SMOOTH SAILING.

DRIVER'S CAP/FLAT CAP

I NEARLY ALWAYS WEAR A HAT LIKE THIS—IT'S CALLED A DRIVER'S CAP OR A FLAT CAP, AND BECAUSE THEY'RE EXPENSIVE, YOU CAN IMAGINE MY EAGERNESS FOR A DO-IT-YOURSELF ALTERNATIVE. FOR THIS ONE, I TORE OUT SEVERAL SHEETS OF ALUMINUM FOIL AND FORMED THEM ON MY HEAD UNTIL THEY RETAINED THE APPROPRIATE SHAPE. THEN, WHILE THE FOIL WAS STILL ON MY HEAD, I MADE A FEW QUICK PLACEMENTS OF TAPE TO HOLD ITS SHAPE. I CAREFULLY PLACED MORE TAPE UNTIL THE HAT WAS COMPLETELY COVERED. MY ADVICE IS TO MAKE IT FIT YOUR HEAD SNUGLY, BUT TO HAVE MORE MATERIAL EXTENDING DOWN AROUND THE EDGES UNTIL THE HAT IS COMPLETE, BECAUSE IT'S ALWAYS EASIER TO SUBTRACT MATERIAL THAN TO ADD IT.

BOOKMARK

THIS BOOKMARK IS RATHER SIMPLE. MORE COMPLICATED VERSIONS INVOLVE SEALING A WIRE OR RIBBON IN THE TAPE SO THAT IT PROTRUDES OUT FROM THE TOP OF THE BOOK. YOU MAY ALSO WANT TO DECORATE THE BOOKMARK WITH IMAGES FROM YOUR FAVORITE BOOK. THIS BOOKMARK IS INSPIRED BY VINCENT VAN GOGH'S *STARRY NIGHT* PAINTING (AS SO MUCH OF MY WORK IS).

DOG LEASH

THE DOG LEASH IS ESSENTIALLY THE SAME AS A STRAIGHT BELT, BUT WITH A CLASP INSTEAD OF A BUCKLE. I DECORATED MINE WITH PAW PRINTS, BUT YOU'RE FREE TO DECORATE HOWEVER YOU WISH. I REINFORCED THE ATTACHMENT POINT OF THE LOOP WITH WIRE, BUT STAPLES ARE ALSO EFFECTIVE.

PENNANT FLAG

THIS IS PRETTY STRAIGHTFORWARD: I MADE A SHEET OF TAPE WITH ABOUT 1 ½ INCHES (3.8 CM) OF ADHESIVE ON ONE SIDE, CUT OUT A PENNANT SHAPE, AND DECORATED IT WITH A CIRCLE AND A STRIPE. THEN, I WRAPPED THE STICKY SIDE AROUND THE POLE. I TRIED TO PICK A PATTERN THAT DOESN'T SIGNIFY ANYTHING IN PARTICULAR—ANY RESEMBLANCE TO REAL-WORLD FLAGS OR SYMBOLS IS PURELY COINCIDENTAL.

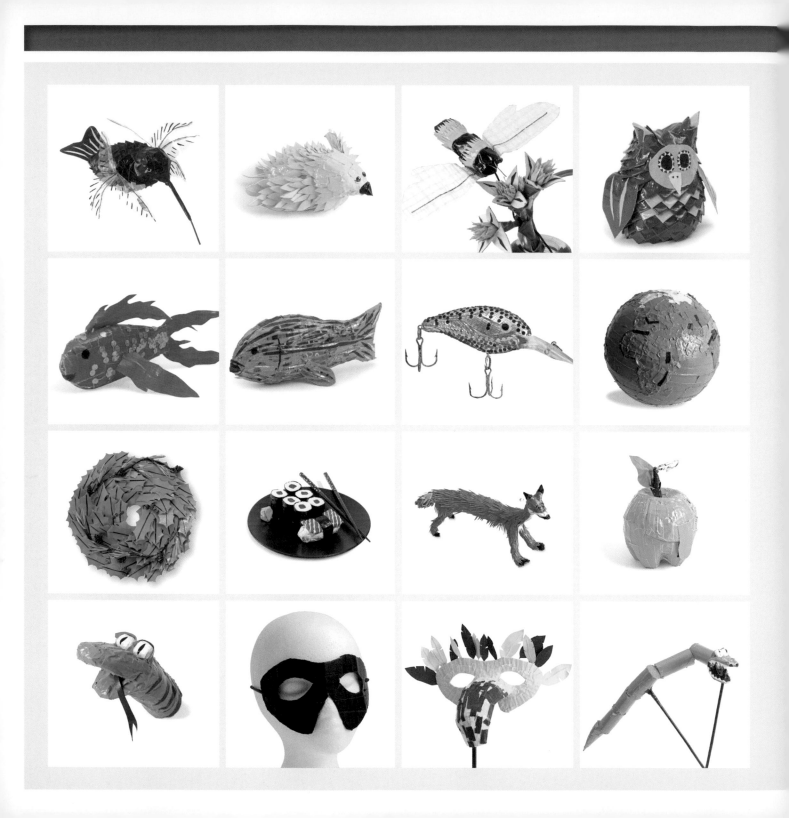

CHAPTER FIVE:
SCULPTURES

"SCULPTURE" MAY NOT FULLY APPLY TO ALL OF THESE ITEMS (OR REALLY, ANY OF THEM, BECAUSE TAPE IS NOT SCULPTED), BUT THEY ARE ALL THREE-DIMENSIONAL ARTWORKS. FOR THE UNDERLYING STRUCTURE, I USED CARDBOARD, PAPER, PLASTIC BAGS, RECYCLED BOTTLES, LEAD FISHING SINKERS, AND OTHER THINGS. FOR LARGER ARTWORKS THAN THE ONES IN THIS BOOK, I'VE USED PVC PIPE, POLYETHYLENE FOAM SHEETS, CHICKEN WIRE, AND PLYWOOD.

HUMMINGBIRD

I FORMED THE BASE MATERIAL FOR THE HUMMINGBIRD (WHICH HAPPENS TO BE THE STUFFING FROM AN OLD PAIR OF SLIPPERS) AROUND A VERY LONG WIRE —LONGER THAN I WOULD ORDINARILY NEED FOR THE ELONGATED BEAK. THE REASON FOR THIS IS THAT THE BEAK WIRE BECOMES THE STEM OF A FLOWER, SO THAT IT LOOKS LIKE THE HUMMINGBIRD IS DRINKING NECTAR.

CANARY

THE FEATHERS FOR THE CANARY ARE ESSENTIALLY
TINY LILY PETALS. I DID NOT PUT WIRES IN THE
FEATHERS BECAUSE IT WOULD HAVE TAKEN A
GHASTLY AMOUNT OF TIME, BUT IN RETROSPECT,
I WOULD HAVE LIKED TO DO SO FOR THE "FLIGHT
FEATHERS" IN THE WINGS AND TAIL.

BUMBLEBEES

THE BUMBLEBEES ARE MADE BY ROLLING DUCT TAPE AROUND THE END OF A WIRE (SEALING TWO SMALL WIRES IN FOR THE ANTENNAE), DECORATING WITH VERY SMALL STRIPS OF "SHORT GRASS STYLE" TAPE, AND FINISHING WITH WINGS MADE FROM CLEAR DUCT TAPE (THE CROSS THREADS OF THE CLEAR DUCT TAPE HAD A SURPRISINGLY REALISTIC EFFECT).

OWL

THE INTERIOR OF THIS OWL IS CRUMPLED-UP PIECES OF NOTEBOOK PAPER, FORMED INTO A ROUGH OVAL SHAPE WITH A FLAT BOTTOM. NEXT, I COVERED THE PAPER IN A PRIMER OF BROWN TAPE. THEN I MADE POINT PETALS 1/4 INCH (6 MM) IN SIZE, ARRANGING THEM IN ROWS FROM THE BOTTOM TO THE TOP. WHEN I GOT TO THE TOP, I FINISHED WITH 1/2-INCH (12 MM) POINT PETALS FOR THE EARS AND CUT OUT TRIANGLES AND CIRCLES WITH A CRAFT KNIFE FOR THE EYES.

GOLDFISH

I THOUGHT ABOUT MAKING ROUNDED LILY PETALS
FOR THE SCALES OF THE GOLDFISH, BUT DECIDED
THAT USING THE HOLE PUNCH WOULD GIVE A SIMILAR
VISUAL EFFECT WITH LESS TIME AND LABOR. THE
FINS ARE FIXED WITH WIRES.

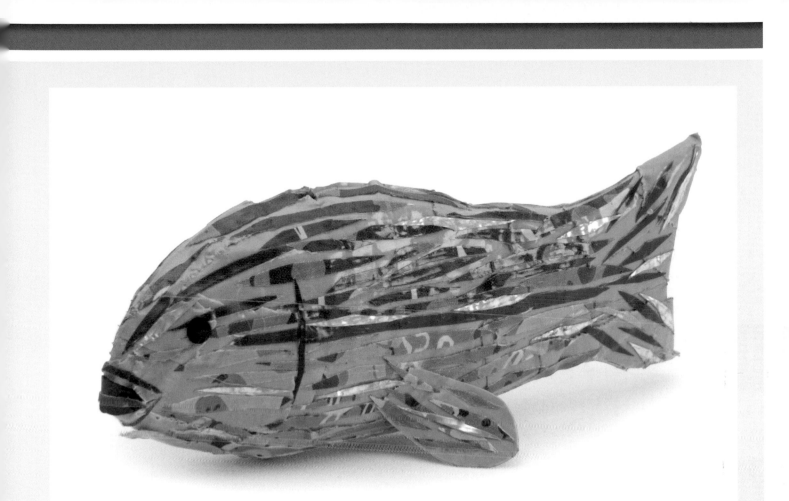

TROUT

THIS IS A BROOK TROUT. THE COLORATION COMES FROM
CAREFULLY SELECTING AND CUTTING OUT THE DARKER AND
LIGHTER COLORS FROM THE SKULL-AND-CROSSBONES PATTERN
OF DUCT TAPE. I DO THIS SORT OF THING A LOT WHEN THE ONLY
SOURCE OF A DESIRED COLOR IS AS PART OF A PATTERN.

MOBILE

THIS IS MY SECOND ATTEMPT AT A MOBILE. THE STRINGS ON THE FIRST ONE (FISHING LINE IN BOTH CASES) WERE TOO LONG, AND IT PROVED DIFFICULT TO ADJUST THE WEIGHT BECAUSE OF THE COMPLICATED SHAPES I'D USED. I HAD SOME HEAVY LEAD WIRES AND SINKERS IN THE FISHING TACKLE BOX THAT I USED TO MAKE THE SMALLER CIRCLES HEAVIER THAN THE LARGE CIRCLES.

FISHING LURE

THIS IS AN OLD FISHING LURE, WHICH I REFURBISHED WITH DUCT TAPE RATHER THAN TRYING TO MAKE A LURE FROM SCRATCH. I'VE COATED IT WITH AN EPOXY TO MAKE IT WATERPROOF. WHEN MY BROTHER RETURNS FROM HIS FISHING TRIP, HE'LL TELL ME WHETHER IT'S AN EFFECTIVE PROJECT OR JUST AN AESTHETIC ONE. EITHER WAY, I LIKE USING DUCT TAPE ART AS A WAY TO RECYCLE AND REFURBISH OLD THINGS AND BRING THEM NEW USE.

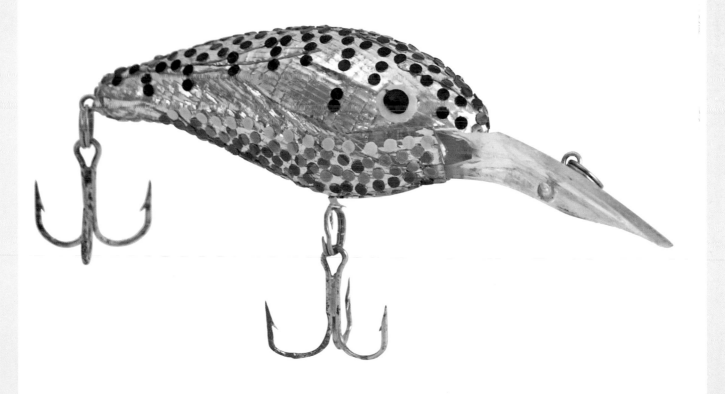

VASE

THIS VASE/DECORATED JAR SEEMS SIMPLE, BUT IT'S ACTUALLY AN ELEGANT WAY TO PREVENT GLASS SHARDS FROM GETTING EVERYWHERE WHEN YOU BREAK SOMETHING. IF YOU WERE TO DROP A GLASS JAR COATED WITH DUCT TAPE, THE GLASS PIECES STICK TO THE DUCT TAPE, MAKING IT SAFER AND EASIER TO CLEAN UP.

GLOBE

THE BASE FOR THIS GLOBE IS A SPHERE OF STYROFOAM THAT I PURCHASED AT A CRAFT STORE. I'VE ALWAYS LIKED MAPS AND GLOBES, SO I CONSIDERED IT A PERSONAL CHALLENGE TO TRY TO COLOR IN THE DETAILS FROM MEMORY.

HOLIDAY WREATH

THIS WREATH WAS PROBABLY ONE OF THE MOST LABOR-INTENSIVE PROJECTS I'VE EVER DONE. THE BACK OF THE WREATH IS A PAPER LANTERN PURCHASED AT A CRAFT STORE. IT'S COMPRISED OF SEVERAL CONCENTRIC RINGS OF METAL COVERED IN PAPER WITH CROSS STRINGS. IT WAS ABSOLUTELY THE PERFECT THING. ONCE I'D MADE A LEAF, I POKED THE WIRE THROUGH TO THE OTHER SIDE AND TAPED IT IN PLACE. I DID THE SAME THING TO THE PINE BRANCHES AND THE HOLLY BERRIES. THE PINECONES ARE POINT-PETAL-BASED, AND THE NEEDLES ARE BASICALLY THE LONG-GRASS CENTERS (SEE PAGE 44).

SUSHI

WHEN I CONSIDERED FOODS TO MAKE OUT OF DUCT TAPE, SUSHI/SASHIMI WAS MY FIRST THOUGHT. IT USUALLY INVOLVES BRIGHT COLORS AND STARK LINES, UNLIKE SOMETHING LIKE PAELLA, WHICH I IMAGINE WOULD BE MUCH MORE DIFFICULT. FOR THE SALMON SASHIMI, I CRUMPLED A SHEET OF NEWSPAPER AND COVERED IT WITH WHITE STRIPS OF TAPE. I TORE THE STRIPS VERY SMALL TO MINIMIZE THE POINTY EFFECT OF FOLDING LARGER STRIPS OF TAPE OVER A ROUNDED SURFACE. I CALL THESE POINTS "TAPE ELBOWS." THE SUSHI WAS MADE BY ROLLING UP A PAPER SHOPPING BAG INTO A TUBE AND THEN CUTTING IT INTO SIX EQUAL-SIZE SECTIONS, THEN COVERING THEM WITH TAPE OF THE PROPER COLOR.

FOX

THE BASE FOR THIS FOX IS A WIRE FRAME TWISTED INTO A ROUGH QUADRUPED SHAPE. I WRAPPED PLASTIC BAGS AROUND THE WIRES, KEEPING THEM IN PLACE WITH A PRIMER COAT OF ORANGE TAPE. FOR THE HAIR, I FOLDED AND CUT THIN POINTS (SEE SHORT GRASS CENTERS AND LONG-GRASS CENTERS, PAGE 44), USING SHORT GRASS FOR THE LEGS AND NECK, AND LONG GRASS FOR THE TAIL AND BODY.

APPLE-SHAPED CHANGE BOX

THIS IS A CONTAINER THAT YOU MIGHT USE FOR KEEPING SOME LUNCH MONEY OR OTHER SMALL OBJECTS TO CLIP TO A CHILD'S BACKPACK. I STARTED WITH A 1-LITER SODA BOTTLE, CUT OUT THE BOTTOM AND TOP, SQUEEZED THEM TOGETHER, AND THEN COVERED THEM WITH TAPE.

THIS IS A HAND PUPPET DESIGN I MADE WITH SOME OF MY
CLASSES OF MIDDLE SCHOOLERS IN OHIO. IT'S JUST A PAPER
BAG CRUMPLED UP OVER ONE HAND AND COVERED IN A FEW
LAYERS OF DUCT TAPE. YOU COULD MAKE ALMOST ANY KIND OF
CHARACTER OR ANIMAL IN THIS WAY. I MADE A SNAKE.

SNAKE HAND
PUPPET

PLAIN/ MASQUERADE MASK

THIS IS AN EFFECTIVE TEMPLATE FOR ANY MASK YOU'D LIKE TO MAKE. IT IS CARDBOARD COVERED WITH STRIPS OF TAPE. IT'S EASIER TO GET SYMMETRY IF YOU DRAW HALF A MASK ON A FOLDED PIECE OF PAPER FIRST.

TOUCAN MASK

THE NOSE FOR THIS MASK BEGAN AS A PIECE OF
CARDBOARD, FOLDED INTO A ROUGH ARCH SHAPE. TO
FORM THE BENDS, I USED SCISSORS TO CUT TRIANGULAR
INCISIONS ON EITHER SIDE OF THE ARCH, THEN I CLOSED
THE TRIANGULAR GAPS WITH TAPE. THIS FORCES THE
PIECE OF CARDBOARD TO CURVE DOWNWARD. I THEN
CUT THE TIP OF THE NOSE INTO AN ANGLED POINT. YOU
COULD MAKE A SHARPER POINT FOR A BIRD OF PREY
LIKE AN EAGLE, OR A SHORTER NOSE WITH A BOTTOM
SECTION FOR A SONGBIRD. THE FEATHERS ARE MADE
IN THE SAME STYLE AS LILY PETALS (PAGE 27) OR THE
FEATHER EARRINGS (PAGE 76).

MARIONETTE

FOR THIS MARIONETTE, I USED CRUMPLED PLASTIC GROCERY BAGS, WHICH WERE MORE PLIABLE AND MADE ROUNDER SURFACES THAN CRUMPLED PAPER. UNFORTUNATELY, I DISCOVERED THAT IT'S VERY DIFFICULT TO POKE A HOLE THROUGH DOZENS OF LAYERS OF PLASTIC LARGE ENOUGH TO THREAD A STRING. IN THE FUTURE, I MIGHT USE FOAM.

SNAKE CHAIN PUPPET/MUPPET WITH STICKS

THIS PUPPET STARTED AS A DRAGON, AND TURNED INTO A SNAKE AS I WENT ALONG. DON'T BE AFRAID TO GO WITH IT IF YOUR PROJECT STARTS GOING IN AN UNEXPECTED DIRECTION. IT'S MADE OF PAPER-TOWEL CARDBOARD TUBES, FILLED WITH PAPER AND STRUNG TOGETHER WITH FISHING LINE.

CHAPTER SIX:
TABLEAUX

I PREFER TO MAKE TWO-DIMENSIONAL ARTWORKS ON MAT BOARD, BUT YOU CAN SURELY USE WOOD, CANVAS, OR ANY OTHER FLAT SURFACE YOU DESIRE. I ADVISE YOU TO MEASURE YOUR SURFACE TO THE SIZE OF THE FRAME YOU'LL EVENTUALLY USE. NOTE THAT BECAUSE BOTH THE SUBSTRATE MATERIAL AND THE TAPE HAVE THICKNESS, YOU'LL HAVE TO ACCOUNT FOR THIS WHEN PICKING A FRAME. I LIKE TO FIND FRAMES AT THRIFT STORES AND YARD SALES, THEN MAKE A PIECE OF ART TO FIT THE FRAME RATHER THAN MAKING ART AND THEN HIRING SOMEONE TO BUILD A CUSTOM FRAME, WHICH CAN BE EXPENSIVE.

CHROMOSOMES

I WAS GIVEN SOME ROLLS OF TAPE FROM A DIFFERENT TAPE COMPANY THAN THE ONE I ORDINARILY USE, AND FOUND THAT THE TWO BRANDS' YELLOWS AND PURPLES WERE SLIGHTLY DIFFERENT, ALLOWING ME SOME MORE SHADING OPTIONS. IT STARTED AS RANDOM OVERLAPPING LINES, BUT AT SOME POINT, I DECIDED THEY RESEMBLED CHROMOSOMES.

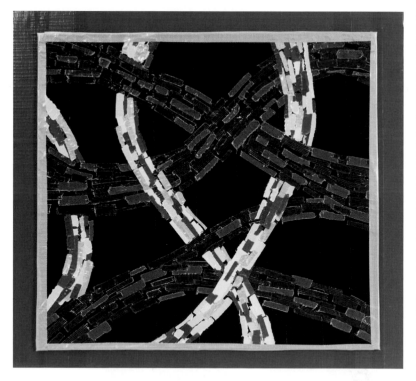

YELLOW LADY

THIS WAS AN EXPERIMENT IN EXAGGERATING FEATURES TO MAKE HER SEEM "CUTE." THE YELLOWNESS IS LESS A FUNCTION OF THIS AND MORE BECAUSE DUCT TAPE HAS YET TO PROVIDE ME WITH MANY REALISTIC FLESH TONES.

MOUNTAINS

THIS LANDSCAPE IS PARTIALLY INSPIRED
BY PAUL CEZANNE, AND IN PART BY SOME
OF THE VISTAS OF THE AMERICAN WEST,
WHERE I NOW LIVE. IF YOU'RE LOOKING
FOR WORK TO EMULATE IN DUCT TAPE,
CEZANNE'S SHORT BRUSHSTROKES ARE A
GOOD PLACE TO START.

PIXILATION

THE TREE IS MADE UP OF "DIGITAL CAMOUFLAGE" PATTERNED DUCT TAPE, WITH THE INDIVIDUAL COLORS CUT OUT AND REARRANGED. THE DESIGNERS OF VIDEO GAMES FROM MY YOUTH USED SPARSE VISUAL RESOURCES TO CREATE ENTIRE WORLDS OUT OF PIXELS, SO THAT MY KID BRAIN HAD NO TROUBLE AT ALL SEEING CARTOON CHARACTERS AND CARS AND BARRELS OUT OF THE SKILLFULLY ARRANGED BLURRY RECTANGLES ON THE SCREEN. YOU CAN MAKE SIMILAR WORK WITH CREATIVE USE OF CIRCLES OR LINES OR CURVES.

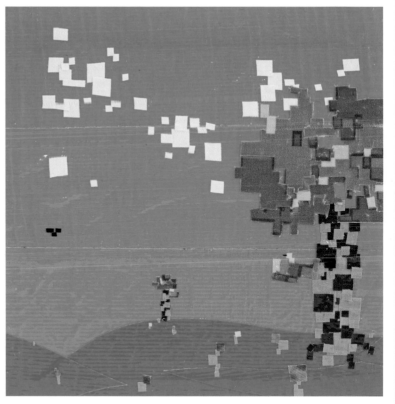

HUMMINGBIRD LADY

THIS IS A FAIRLY STRAIGHTFORWARD PIECE—THE BODY AND WINGS OF THE HUMMINGBIRD WERE CUT IN THEIR ENTIRETY ON THE CUTTING BOARD AND THEN EMBELLISHED WITH THE RED, BLACK, GREEN, TEAL, AND BROWN DETAILS. THE ORANGE TRIANGLES IN THE FLOWER ARE TINY SQUARES (PARALLEL AND PERPENDICULAR LINES WITH A CRAFT KNIFE) CUT DIAGONALLY, AS IN THE SNOWFLAKE EARRINGS (PAGE 70).

STARS

THIS IS ANOTHER VAN GOGH-INSPIRED
PIECE, ONE OF THE FIRST TWO-
DIMENSIONAL ARTWORKS THAT I EVER
MADE WITH DUCT TAPE, CIRCA 2005.
THE BACKGROUND IS TORN STRIPS,
AND THE FOREGROUND WAS MADE WITH
THE CRAFT KNIFE. THE CHROME TAPE
USED FOR THE STARS HAS SINCE FADED
WITH FRICTION, BEFORE I STARTED
USING CLEAR ACRYLIC COATING TO
PREVENT THIS.

QUESTION OF SCALE

WITH THIS PIECE, I WANTED TO DRAW A COMPARISON BETWEEN THINGS THAT ARE INCOMPREHENSIBLY LARGE AND INCREDIBLY SMALL. MUCH OF THIS WAS DONE WITH THE SCREW PUNCH AND THE REST IS FROM THE CRAFT KNIFE. I HAD ALWAYS INTENDED IT TO BE HUNG WITH THE PLANETS PORTION ON TOP AND THE ATOMS PORTION BELOW. THE CENTER QUARTER OF THE PICTURE MARKS A TRANSITION FROM LIGHT STRIPS ON DARK TO DARK STRIPS ON LIGHT, WHICH I HOPED WOULD REMIND THE VIEWER OF M.C. ESCHER'S TRANSITIONS.

PROMETHEUS

PROMETHEUS WAS A GREEK GOD WHO BROUGHT FIRE FROM MOUNT OLYMPUS TO THE MEN OF EARTH. I IMAGINED THIS AS A FIRE-HAIRED MAN WITH A SPHERE OF ENERGY. THE SPHERE IS MADE OF GLOW-IN-THE-DARK TAPE. THE CURL FROM MAKING ARCS WITH TAPE IS PARTICULARLY NOTICEABLE HERE; THIS CAN BE REDUCED BY MAKING A SMALL SLIT IN THE OUTER EDGE OF THE CURVE AND BRIDGING THE GAP WITH AN ADDITIONAL DAUB OF TAPE. THIS CAN BE TIME-CONSUMING; YOUR MILEAGE MAY VARY.

NEON SPIRAL

THIS SPIRAL WAS MADE BY TEARING STRIPS AND LAYING THEM HORIZONTALLY ON A PIECE OF THIN PLASTIC (IT CAME FROM A CONTAINER OF COOKIES), THEN CUTTING THE SHAPES AND CAREFULLY PEELING THEM FROM THE PLASTIC SCRAPS. THIS TECHNIQUE IS USEFUL FOR MAKING COLORFUL LETTERS OR FLOWER PETALS AND MUCH MORE.

PAISLEY LADY

TO MAKE THIS PICTURE, I PLACED STRIPS OF GRAY TAPE ON A CARDBOARD SURFACE IN THE SHAPE OF AN OVAL, THEN MARKED THE PLACES ON THE OVAL WHERE THE EYES, NOSE, AND LIPS WOULD BE. NEXT, I STACKED DOZENS OF STRIPS OF TAPE ON THE "TALLEST" PARTS OF THE FACE (TIP OF THE NOSE, CHIN, CHEEKBONES, AND FOREHEAD), LEAVING LESS MATERIAL ON THE LOWER PARTS OF THE EYES AND EDGE OF THE FACE, AS IT RECEDES TOWARD THE BACK OF THE HEAD. LAST, I FINISHED THE PICTURE WITH COLORED TAPE, CREATING A WORK WITH DEPTH.

ALBUM COVER

I HAVE MADE TWO ALBUM COVERS FOR MUSICAL FRIENDS. THIS IS ONE (FRONT AND BACK) I DID FOR MY FRIEND ANDREW BONNIS. I WAS INSPIRED BY ONE OF MY FORMER STUDENTS, WHO DID SOME BEAUTIFUL WORK REPLICATING HER FAVORITE ALBUM COVERS IN DUCT TAPE.

POINT-CIRCLE

I'VE MADE A NUMBER OF VERSIONS OF THIS, BUT THIS ONE IS THE LARGEST. IT TOOK SEVERAL WEEKS TO TEAR ALL THE SQUARES AND FOLD AND PLACE THEM. LUCKILY, I HAD SOME HELP. I STARTED BY MAKING THE BACKGROUND, THEN I DREW A CIRCLE. I TRIED TO KEEP THE POINTS EVENLY SPACED AS I WENT AROUND THE CIRCLE, LINING UP THE POINTS WITH THE CIRCLE I'D DRAWN AND GOING STEADILY TOWARD THE CENTER. WHEN I NEARED THE MIDDLE, I SWITCHED FROM FULL-SIZE SQUARES TO HALF-SIZE, THEN QUARTER- AND EIGHTH-SIZE SQUARES.

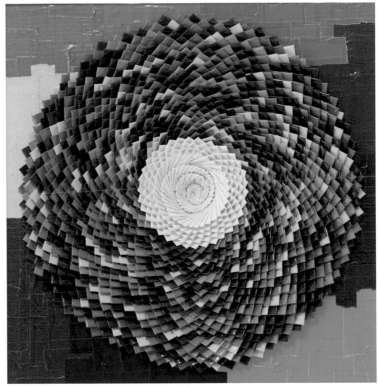

RESOURCES

www.duckbrand.com
The Duck Brand maintains a great website, with sections on where to buy tape, contests, and project ideas. You can see their whole selection, and order directly from the site. The FAQ section is also a great place to head for answers to your tape-related questions.

www.deviantart.com
Deviant Art is an enormous global community of artists posting art voluntarily to various galleries. Searching for "Duck Tape", "Duct Tape" or "Tape Art" will give you thousands of ideas for interesting projects. Keep in mind, though, that you should always be careful about using others' ideas—use them as inspiration, but don't duplicate.

www.michaels.com
www.joann.com
www.patcatans.com
Craft stores like Michael's, JoAnn Fabrics, and Pat Catan's are great places to buy not only tape, but also other materials like wire, foam, jewelry backings, and tools.

Other Materials:
Much of the materials that make up the structure of your artwork can be found around you for free—cardboard boxes, paper, discarded wires, and plastic bottles. It is always a good idea to make friends with tradespeople like carpenters, plumbers, and electricians because they often have useful scraps.

There are many people I would like to thank. I am tremendously lucky to have had a wonderful tribe of human beings who nurtured and encouraged and helped me in some way. Tragically, no matter how long I make this list, it's doomed to be incomplete. I am sure that as soon as I submit this to the publisher, I will smack my forehead in shame for excluding someone important. I'll make every effort to correct this eventually.

ACKNOWLEDGMENTS

My mom and dad, Clare and Jim, whose help is incalculable and ongoing, and who remain my favorite people and my best role models forever.

My brother, Clay, the best little brother anyone ever had.

My cousins, grandparents, uncles, and aunts.

ShurTech Brands, marketers of Duck brand duct tape.

The Fine Arts Association of Willoughby and Wickliffe Middle School, and all my students who taught me more than you'll know.

Richard Gallup and Gallup's Fine Art.

Cliff Novak and Kirtland High School.

Mick Briscoe.

Quarry Books, and Jonathan Simcosky for his patience.

Matt Hunsaker.

Brook Castle-Goins.

Andrew Bonnis , Leah Lou & The Two Left Shoes.

Chris Stoicovici.

Leah McCoy.

Stan and Nancy Pavelecky.

The Coles family.

Ted Burtt.

Jamie Jelenic and Rachel Olson, for letting me make art for your weddings.

Greg Harrison and the other Enclavians.

Lakeland Community College.

My workshops and their staffs and owners:

OHIO:

Borders Mentor

Barnes and Noble Mentor

Rick Fox and the Kirtlander

Negative Space

Fuel

Java Express

Algebra

Gypsy Bean

Phoenix

The Fairmount Bar

The Bottlehouse

Blue Planet Coffee

Center Perk

OREGON:

Bluebird Coffee

Dudley's

Backporch

McMenamins

VERMONT:

Langdon Street Café

Basement Teen Center and the WCYSB

ABOUT THE AUTHOR

Forest grew up in a suburb of Cleveland, Ohio, where he learned a love of the arts from his musician father and artist mother. He has taught duct tape art classes at the Willoughby Fine Arts Association, and, through them, at various schools in northeast Ohio. He has on occasion been commissioned to do artwork for the Duck brand, participating in the annual Duck Tape Festival in Avon, Ohio, and has made art for several album covers and two weddings.

In addition to his artwork, he enjoys playing music, cooking, making beer, and participating in pub trivia challenges. He is currently living with his brother, brother's girlfriend, and cousin in Bend, Oregon, where he works at a coffee shop and enjoys the natural beauty of the high desert.

ALSO AVAILABLE

Washi Tape
ISBN: 978-1-59253-914-7

Art Without Waste
ISBN: 978-1-63159-031-3

Playing with Paper
ISBN: 978-1-59253-814-0

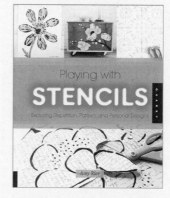

Playing with Stencils
ISBN: 978-1-59253-829-4